TABLE OF CONT

Table of contents

KRATOM

How We Met | Meeting Kratom

The First Kratom Package – and how it romanced me.

The Science Behind My Alkaloid Romance | What is Kratom?

What Most Unsuspecting People Use Kratom for

How Kratom is Taken

How Deceit Bonded Our Relationship | The First Lie About Kratom

How Kratom Solved My Drinking Problem

How Kratom Gave Me a False Sense of Happiness

One Day I Woke Up & I Was Suddenly a Kratom Addict

Why We Broke Up | The Many Reasons I Ended My Relationship with Kratom | When it's Time to Quite Kratom

Negative Side Effects of Kratom

What Happens When You Stop Taking Kratom

The Physical Issues Still With me 8 Months into Recovery

The Positives of Quitting Kratom

Kratom Informative – What You Need to Know About Kratom

Quitting Kratom Using Tapering

Quitting Kratom Cold Turkey

The Rehab Route

Using Agmatine and Black Seed Oil – Viable or Not?

Kratom Hair Loss – Why it Happens, What to Expect, & What to do About it

How to Heal Your Kratom Induced Thyroid Problems

Kratom and Sexy Time Obliteration

Kratom & Digestive Problems

Kratom and Anorexia

Holistic Natural Supplements to Ease Kratom Cravings

Doctor Prescribed Medications Often Used in Recovery

The risk of depression and suicidal thoughts

Stare Relapse in the Face | Managing Relapse

The End, or is it?

KRATOM

If you type "what is Kratom?" into a Google search, a variety of options will be spat out at you. Some sources merely explain that Kratom is a plant and go on to say where it originates from. Others tell of the plant's ability to help serious drug addicts overcome their addictions and stave off the desire to overindulge in a hard-core drug of choice (usually heroin). Other posts simply sing the praises of it and claim it is a miracle plant for a number of reasons.

One particular heading that catches my eye and rings true in *my* life is "Kratom: unsafe and ineffective" and I am drawn to it. Mostly because I didn't seem to come across headlines like this when I was pro-Kratom – or perhaps I just turned a blind eye while elbows deep in denial? I didn't always feel this way about Kratom and for a long time, I might have rolled my eyes and even argued that it's an "obviously uninformed title". To tell you the truth, there was a point where I sung its praises, read up on it almost obsessively, introduced people to it, and was in total awe of it.

Kratom has a way of making you become obsessed with it. And once that had happened to me; I started over-using it, hiding it, lying about it, and choosing to be in denial about it. In my opinion – which is stuck gloriously in hindsight – if you have to deny or lie about something, it's generally not right. The story of my relationship with Kratom doesn't have a happy ending (for me and Kratom that is). While it was a relationship that started off with the type of honeymoon phase no one can ever dream of forgetting, the havoc it eventually wreaked in my life has all but stripped that fond feeling you get with happy memories from both my heart and mind.

Before I tried Kratom, I never really believed in "natural" or herbal medications and treatments. I never truly believed that they worked. I thought they were ineffective. If someone offered me a "natural alternative" for an ailment I was suffering, I would forego it and seek out a prescription for chemical drugs – you know; the real thing. I've never believed that mere plants could do the things people claimed they could – which is mildly bizarre considering I am a vegan - and then Kratom changed my mind. Kratom wooed me. Kratom made the world feel right. Kratom was always there to lift a bad mood, quell a misplaced emotion, and calm an angry thought process. Before I knew it, Kratom was my go-to and just when I thought that I could exist in the Kratom-induced love bubble for eternity, it turned on me, sucked the wind out of my proverbial sails and hurt me. Think of the biggest emotional betrayal of your life and you will understand how Kratom didn't just bring me down…it brought me to my knees to such an extent that I was begging for normalcy.

When researching for this e-book, I asked connections on Kratom to give me some feedback on their views on the drug and recovery. One particular comment that really spoke to me was made by Reddit user (ratearther) and I must share it because it really resonates:

"Kratom is so deeply polarized as a miracle plant or surefire gateway to the classic opiates. It sort of makes sense, because the body of clinical research on the plant is so small…most of our assumptions about its supposed risks and benefits are largely anecdotal. It's such a pharmacologically strange and complex drug and I think we under-appreciate the extent that confounding variables (especially related to our mental health, drug interactions etc) play into addiction, withdrawals, and general responses to Kratom." – ratearther (Reddit)

HOW WE MET | MEETING KRATOM

I met Kratom in the final stages of 2016. As an anxiety sufferer, I am always looking around for miracle cures to my affliction. But that's not the only reason I met Kratom. I was also going through a particularly difficult relationship situation at the time and looking for ways to calm my nerves and "take the edge off" so to speak. In 2016, my go-to was alcohol - to stave off anxiety, which I almost always feel in social settings. It was also my go-to to calm my over-active mind – I am a thinker (scratch that – I am an OVER-thinker).

At the time, my social life was taking a few awkward turns. My group encounters were increasing and thus, so was my binge drinking. The problem is this ... while everyone else thinks I am a fun time when I drink alcohol, I hate that person the person I become. The person that says stupid things, fights with her partner, and ends up falling around, slurring, shouting to be heard (I have seen and heard the videos) and generally just being a societal fart. I hate that girl and I desperately wanted it to stop, but I didn't really want to give up the happy social buzz that alcohol tends to give me. I spent quite a few weeks considering strategic plans for giving up the booze without having to give up my social life too. I also had to be quite selective as I was taking an anti-depressant.

I am not over-exaggerating when I say that I put hours and days into thinking about it. I started amping up my online research, looking for information. I was obsessively looking for advice on how to cure my social anxiety, still enjoy socialising, and not have to become a drunken fool to do so.

And then I saw it – mentions of Kratom. A substance I had *never* heard of. I encountered forum after forum about how Kratom helped alcoholics kick the habit. I saw even more posts on how people use Kratom for socialising with "absolutely zero negative side effects". In fact, many of the posts I was reading claimed that Kratom helped them enjoy hangover-free days where they were more productive and relaxed than ever before. A large portion of the users also claimed that they kicked their anti-depressants to the curb after introducing Kratom to their daily "supplements" schedule. It really did sound like a dream come true – too good to be true even. And when I did some local research, I was delighted to discover that there were (still are) many local suppliers in my country. And so I ordered some online – and that, my fellow Kratom quitters, is where it all began.

The First Kratom Package – and how it romanced me.

For those who have tried or are currently addicted to Kratom, you will know that there are different strains available. As a beginner, you don't know too much about the strains and it's only natural to spend a bit of time testing them all out. Even the information provided online doesn't truly live up to the true feeling of amazesome that Kratom can make a user feel. Of course, Google and Reddit were my best friends in finding out as much as I could. I read a lot of good things about red strains and green strains being excellent for euphoria and energy - naturally, those are what I wanted to try out first.

My first order I will never forget. It was in fact the one that changed the entire trajectory of my life. In my mind (the addicted mind that is) my brain seems to have romanticised that first order to the point where I still see it and look back on it "through rose tinted glasses". That only goes to speak to the power of the human addicted mind.

I ordered a red strain and a green strain. The afternoon that it arrived, I opened the package, measured out a scoop of the earthy-smelling greenish powder, mixed it in some water and drank it down. I was keen to try this uplifting mood enhancing powder – after all, I had just had the fight of the year with my partner that morning and was all twisted up inside. It tasted repulsive (no romance there!). I didn't really feel anything immediately and so shrugged it off as one of those "ineffective herbal treatments" and went about my day with mild disappointment at the money lost.

About 20 minutes later, I felt it. And I will never forget it. It felt like a warm flood was gently washing over my entire body. I took what felt like a luxuriously deep breath and that's when it hit me. The feeling that can only be described in the following words: "everything is absolutely 100% right with the world". I had read the term "sense of well-being" in many Kratom reviews and didn't really understand what people were talking about, until that warm wave washed over me and I felt it for myself. It's a truly indescribable feeling. And best of all, I was still completely in control of my body. That's one of the perks of Kratom. I found that I could be experiencing the most amazing sense of euphoria and well-being and unlike other drugs, I was completely in control of my body and my actions. It's truly transformational. And of course, makes it easy to be high around others without them ever knowing (wink).

As someone with anxiety, and the fact that I was currently in the middle of some pretty crap relationship problems, that feeling provided a sense of relief to such immense intensity that I don't even know if I can describe it in words. I could probably paint some pretty epic abstract paintings in its honour – yes, I was that in love with it. Everything seemed so okay, more okay than ever before. It wasn't like I knew it was a false (or unreal) feeling though. Like when you take shrooms and you're drawn into the world around you, but you still KNOW it isn't real. It's not like that with Kratom – you believe it's real and I only know that now in hindsight. I was absolutely convinced that everything was in fact 100% perfect in life. It genuinely felt as if everything had suddenly just become perfectly okay and I was happy, content, at ease. All the stresses and strains melted away. I wasn't even angry at my partner anymore – his decisions and harsh words no longer hurt. I felt like I had the ability to overcome anything really.

If you haven't tried it before, here's what you need to know about the nature of Kratom. Kratom is not like cannabis, ecstasy, MDMA, or any other recreational drug you might have tried. It's a very timid drug that has a far greater impact than you even know it is having. For a drug to make you feel that immense sense of wellbeing, without making you absolutely high off your rocker – that's skill. And that's a sheer testament to the power of this particular drug. It's not a temperamental drug – it's controlled. Worst of all is that you don't know that while you are enjoying that feeling, Kratom is taking control of you. Not just on a surface level. It is digging deep into your soul and getting a foothold. And every time you use it, Kratom digs its claws just a little deeper.

The Science Behind My Alkaloid Romance | What is Kratom?

Wikipedia defines Kratom as follows:

"Mitragyna speciosa is a tropical evergreen tree in the coffee family native to Southeast Asia. M. speciosa is indigenous to Thailand, Indonesia, Malaysia, Myanmar, and Papua New Guinea, where it has been used in traditional medicines since at least the nineteenth century."

What we know about Kratom is that it is native to South East Asia. Its leaves contain compounds and alkaloids that have mind-altering (or psychotropic) effects on humans. People who become addicted to Kratom are usually addictive to the stimulant and euphoric effects that the drug has. The alkaloids are what are responsible for the stimulating, mood-altering, and pain relieving effects that Kratom has on the brain.

How Kratom affects the brain can be complex to explain and I don't want to confuse anyone. In simple terms, I can explain it as follows. When Kratom is consumed, it can have the same effects as stimulants and opioids. Think of Heroin and its effects – Heroin is an opioid made from Morphine. So Kratom has similar effects to Heroin. The leaves of the plant contain two rather powerful compounds as follows:

- Mitragynine
- 7-a-hydroxymitragynine

These compounds actually pay a visit to the brain and seek out the opioid receptors where they do most of their work. The result of this visit is:

- Sedation
- Pleasure (feelings of pleasure)
- Decreased sensitivity or even awareness of pain

- Increased openness and sociability (relaxed and talkativeness are common)
- Sense of wellbeing
- Giddiness
- Increased energy levels
- Alertness
- Ability to focus & concentrate for long periods

Research has been carried out by the United States Food and Drug Administration on Kratom and its potential to be abused. The Commissioner of the FDA, Scott Gottlieb (MD) presented scientific evidence on the presence of opioid compounds in the plant. In fact, he presented his evidence in February 2018 when I was still using the substance quite heavily. You can read his findings here, but I will summarise them below for you:

Kratom is an agonist. It binds to the brain's mu-opioid receptors. This happens to be the very same part of the brain that experiences the "reward" when you take an opioid. For instance, when someone becomes addicted to prescription pain killers or a drug like heroin, it is their mu-opioid receptors that are actually addicted. It's a difficult addiction because the body becomes a slave to the brain. The brain wants the reward and for that to be possible, the user is often willing to abuse their body to great lengths to provide the brain with what it needs. Yep, it's pretty messed up. This being said, Kratom is for all intents and purposes, an opioid, albeit a natural one. All opioids, whether natural or synthetic, come with risks attached. Addiction, dependence, tolerance, and withdrawal are all very similar across the board.

What Most Unsuspecting People Use Kratom for

- Treatment of chronic pain
- Aid for withdrawal from opium dependence
- Treatment of depression
- Treatment of OCD and anxiety
- Treatment of hypertension

Official medical and drug abuse/rehab websites will tell you that there is insufficient information on Kratom to determine its effectiveness in any of these treatments. Drug rehab and treatment centres will tell you that Kratom is legal in some countries and is often used to treat withdrawals but – and to quote one website – "can be just as addictive as opiates".

If you are the type to sneer at medical documents and somehow believe that doctors and medical professionals are speaking out against Kratom because they just don't want you to have fun, or just don't "get" the value of Kratom (all the nay-sayers), or want to make money on mainstream medicines – fine. I have heard all of these excuses before since quitting the substance. But here I am. I am not a medical professional and I am not a doctor. I stand to gain nothing by speaking out against Kratom and I am only doing so, so that others don't suffer the same complications that I did, simply because I would not listen.

There's a quote that goes "don't confuse your Google search with my medical degree" – which really should make us realise that these pros are in their positions for a reason and can be trusted with their negative viewpoints on Kratom. I digress though. I was a nay-sayer for a long time myself. I gave Kratom a chance. I let it be a big part of my life and it nearly destroyed me. If you don't want to take the word of the pros – take *my* word for it. I am walking, talking, evidence that Kratom has some positive results, but the negatives far outweigh the positives.

How Kratom is Taken

I, personally, only ever bought Kratom in capped form (already packed into capsules) or in a powder form that you can "toss and wash" or mix in with some water and swallow it down. Some people get creative and put it in smoothies, but I could never stomach the taste, so I would pop my scoop measure into a small container, add water, shake it around a bit and then drink it like a shot at a bar – complete with "tequila face" too. Everyone has their personal style and I can quite confidently say that a lot of users see their method of consuming Kratom as somewhat of a ritual. This is probably because a user has to re-dose several times a day. We all get into our habits.

Kratom is available in the following forms:

- Compressed pills
- Powder extracts
- Capsules

Some may choose to chew the leaves, or make a tea from it. Unfortunately, some commercial forms of Kratom that have been tested have been found to be laced with a number of other compounds – some of which have caused death. Luckily, this is not something that I encountered. One thing to note – if you *are* going to try Kratom…never, ever try to snort it. That is a whole world of pain and displeasure you just don't want to get yourself into!

How Deceit Bonded Our Relationship | The First Lie About Kratom

The first lie I ever told about Kratom was to my partner and I will never forgive myself for the lies that seemed to tumble out of me so easily in the months to follow that first mis-truth.

At this stage I had only used Kratom a handful of times and was still trying to get my doses right, which really was a touch and go situation for me – I was useless in the beginning. On one occasion I took Kratom (which I had told him was for anxiety, which I believed it was) before going to a party. Before we arrived at the party, my head was spinning, my stomach was desperately upset and I was vomiting. I had taken too much Kratom too quickly. I had to go home, which ended in an argument and of course, me missing out on an evening of fun.

On another occasion, I took Kratom before one of his work functions and all seemed to be going well. And then someone handed me a glass of red wine. I had been avoiding alcohol completely while using Kratom, as I actually felt no need to drink while using it. If you remember correctly, this is the precise reason I wanted to take Kratom in the first place and I felt ever so lucky that it was working out perfectly by this stage. But when the glass of wine was passed to me, I couldn't refuse and I drank it. And then something terrible happened. I completely lost my sense of self. My head was spinning and I became aggressive. I was extremely drunk on less than half a glass and I proceeded to fight viciously with him in front of his work colleague, which is very out of character for me. The night ended badly. Separate bedrooms for us that night!

After this second occasion, my partner decided to investigate for himself, secretly I might add, what I was using and he was not happy or impressed with what he had found. He presented me with pages of information he had found, questions about opioid addiction, questions about lies (when and how was I getting this drug) – so many questions! Needless to say, he wanted me to stop immediately as he felt that while Kratom is used to help people with opioid addictions, it too is addictive in much the same way and was impacting on my behaviour somewhat. I told him I wasn't aware of all the dangers he had looked up and that I would stop. Unfortunately, that wasn't quite the truth. I had done a lot of reading and knew the controversy around the substance…but that's Kratom for you. It doesn't ask you to lie – you just find yourself lying to protect it. After that night, I had every intention of stopping, but I didn't. And I proceeded to hide my use from him for over a year longer. There's a little quote that pops into my head every time I think back on these lies and it goes "the devil doesn't lie; he equivocates". It seems so apt.

How Kratom Solved My Drinking Problem

As I intended to use Kratom instead of drinking, that is exactly what I did. Even after my partner had discovered I was using a potentially dangerous drug and knew I was replacing alcohol with it and wanted me to stop, I continued to do it – behind his back. I used it and simply told people I was cutting back on drinking. My ability to "cut back on booze" was seemingly impressive to others. I continued though, I am ashamed to say.

All I can say is that when you are hiding the use of a substance from a loved one (your partner especially), it's probably a sure-fire sign that you are becoming, or already are, addicted. Well… I loved it and at this stage, I had no intention of giving it up. Relationship be damned and all that. I don't feel that way anymore.

White Kratom strains were my social buzz. I felt more talkative on it and I felt the most amazing euphoria when using it. Nothing my partner said upset me, everyone was wonderful – life was wonderful. And so my drinking ceased. Which was great – I won't lie. I went several months without touching a drop of alcohol. Yet in my handbag was my little container of Kratom and on a night out, all I did was dose and re-dose my way through the night. Drinking problem solved, right?

How Kratom Gave Me a False Sense of Happiness

While I was living in a haze of well-being thanks to my Kratom use – everything was wonderful. Nothing upset me. I felt more relaxed and I was able to get work and personal projects done with enjoyment. Kratom had introduced a whole new way of living to me.

There was only one glitch; I only felt this sense of happiness and well-being *while* using the Kratom. When I didn't have any, the old feelings of unhappiness, anxiety, stress, frustration – they all came back. The only way to get these feelings to dissipate was to pop a few grams of Kratom. The happiness and sense of well-being that I felt while using Kratom was wonderful, but it wasn't real. It was just masking what I was really feeling and that in itself is dangerous. The problem is that it's a believable feeling of happiness. You don't ever get a sense that it's not real. And that's why you don't really blink an eye at the situation: you are using a drug to make you feel better, so what could possibly be wrong with that? This is the very reason why so many people use Kratom as a "natural" form of anti-depressant.

If Kratom made one feel this way without any negative physical and psychological impacts, I would probably be prone to say "go for it". What's not to love, right? The problem is that Kratom does wreak physical, emotional, and psychological havoc on a person. Because there are no in-depth studies released, people choose to be blind and live in denial. While this isn't a medically researched or official psychological study, I and many other ex-kratom users are proof that it has an evil side – and everyone should be careful of it.

One Day I Woke Up & I Was Suddenly a Kratom Addict

In the beginning, I remember telling my supplier that I only intended on using Kratom for social events and on weekends. She said to me it was absolutely safe to do so and just to make sure that I take a "break" day here and there or I will develop a tolerance for the drug. There was never any mention of the dangers of the drug – in fact, I had never heard a single negative thing about it from those supplying me with it. Since I have quit, I have tried to discuss the negative impact it has had on me with suppliers, who have outright ignored me.

What started out as weekend use eventually morphed into tri-weekly use, and by January of 2019 I was strategically heading to the bathroom at least every 2 hours (sometimes far less) to quickly chug the dose I desperately needed just to feel normal. I wasn't even feeling that sense of well-being or euphoria anymore. I just needed the fix to feel mildly okay. What happened to me? How did I get there? What changed the non-addicted girl I was into someone who couldn't even get through 2 hours without a 2gram dose of Kratom? And why wasn't my Kratom working anymore? When you suddenly realise you are taking 14 grams a day and it's no longer getting you that sense of well-being you used to feel – you realise you have a problem. Just before I finally quit, I realised that I was perpetually chasing a feeling that I was never going to feel again and the negative physical discomforts I was willing to go through, just to do that day after day, simply weren't worth it.

Why We Broke Up | The Many Reasons I Ended My Relationship with Kratom | When it's Time to Quite Kratom

By the time I quit Kratom, this is what had happened (these reasons all added up are what spurred me on to finally say no to the Kratom addiction I was choosing to support). Please note, these are personal side effects and results, every user has a unique experience and outcomes:

- My digestive system was completely messed up – in short, I was pooping painful gushes of blood.
- My kidneys were taking strain and ached – my eyes were yellow, and urinating had become more of a regular challenge than just something that's done every day. The kidneys are put under a lot of strain when constantly filtering out toxins.
- I was starting to feel tired and uninspired all the time.
- My weight dropped to 42kg and I lacked an interest in food. I sometimes didn't eat the entire day in hopes that it would fuel the strength of my Kratom.
- I was out of breath when trying to do any form of physical exercise – even a short walk down the path.
- I started to isolate myself, rather not being around people (massive mood swings).
- I started needing more and more Kratom, which started costing money. When I took more Kratom and didn't get the desired effects (my tolerance had become quite strong), I became moody, irrational, frustrated, irritated, easily annoyed, depressed.
- I had several fights with my partner in public due to mixing Kratom and alcohol (not a good mix for me). I have read others also say that mixing Kratom and alcohol gets them drunk super-fast. Well, me too!
- My sleep patterns were a mess – insomnia ruled me.

- Being unable to keep up with my doses throughout the day and night, I started getting night sweats, headaches, the shakes.
- Without my fix, everyone and everything was annoying, irritating, and frustrating to extremes (something that I don't feel now that I am off Kratom).
- I started missing deadlines at work.
- I eventually got piles from the seemingly incurable constipation and digestive issues that come with Kratom use. I had to take Movicol on a daily basis.
- My skin became very dry regardless of how much I hydrated and moisturized. People would comment that I had dark rings under my eyes and looked tired. I started looking my age (never been the case before) and I noticed a lot of fine wrinkles around my eyes.
- The white of my eyes were almost constantly reddish or yellowish.
- My gums started receding and I got what I call "lurgies" in the back of my throat.
- I was getting ulcers on my tongue and an "acid tongue" which doctors investigated and told me is a side-effect of "taking certain medications". I couldn't explain to them that I was taking Kratom and so that remained an "unsolved" mystery.
- I was getting rashes on my neck and chest that stuck around for weeks at a time.
- I had suddenly developed a thyroid problem that I kept explaining away with other potential causes/reasons. Just FYI, months into recovery and my thyroid problems are finally getting better.
- I put myself and my partner at risk while traveling by taking Kratom in my luggage into countries I am not sure have legalized it. I never really checked – all I knew is that I needed to take it with me.

- I started to act cagey because I always had to sneak off for a secret dose. This does nothing for trust in a relationship, by the way.
- I received several courier packages to my home, strategically timed for when my partner wouldn't be around, and labelled as something completely different. I hid my delivered stash in the house, where I thought it would never be found. I believe the act of omission is as bad as a lie – and I was lying to the person I love most.
- I took Kratom every time I felt horrible about something or had an emotional feeling, just so I wouldn't have to feel it (that meant months of problems were just put off and never dealt with).
- I bought Moringa powder (a harmless substance) to keep in the house; just in case my Kratom was discovered (I could then claim it was Moringa). I would pour my Kratom supply into Moringa branded containers.
- I ruined a holiday by being lethargic, suffering massive mood swings, and being extremely nauseous, just because plans had changed and I was unable to get my day's Kratom doses. I also severely overdosed on Kratom while on holiday and was sick and unable to participate in anything for hours.
- Finally, the last straw and probably the most terrifying thing I have experienced in my whole life – my hair started thinning and then falling out in chunks, which is not a great thing for a girl with long brown hair.

Did Kratom cause all of this? I can say without a doubt that it did. And it's the saddest thing in the world for me because all I ever wanted was to keep Kratom as a big part of my life. I fell in love with it. I gave it my trust. And in the end, it gave me total physical disregard. It changed my mind set and set my health back so badly that now while writing this, many months into my sobriety / recovery, I am still struggling to bounce back. Luckily my relationship survived all of this.

I hope this book will help to answer the question of how you can go from using once a week for good intentions (to quit drinking and be a better partner) to being a lying, deceitful partner who hides a drug addiction. I hope you realise that it can happen to you – and I hope that after reading this you choose to make positive changes as I am doing each and every day. If you have already quit or are struggling to quit, I hope that my story and information found on Kratom provides you with a bit of a kick to push on and keep resisting the draw of the leaf!

NEGATIVE SIDE EFFECTS OF KRATOM

If you happen to take a bit too much Kratom, or it just doesn't agree with you (some people have had this happen), then you may experience some horrible side-effects. I have felt all of these at one point or another, usually from over-indulging (naughty, I know).

- Nausea and the effect of head spinning
- Vomiting
- Headaches
- Diarrhoea (not often but can happen the first few times you take too much)
- Sweating
- Constipation
- Increased heart rate
- Decreased or no appetite
- Increased urination
- Itchy skin
- Shakes (some people have had seizures)
- Cotton mouth (dry mouth)
- Extreme sedation (having to sleep immediately)
- Thyroid imbalance
- Aggression
- Obliteration of sex drive and libido
- Uneasy sense.

Lucky, if you manage to throw up and have a good nap, these symptoms will pass in a few hours.

WHAT HAPPENS WHEN YOU STOP TAKING KRATOM

When you stop taking Kratom, especially if it has become a regular thing, the body goes into withdrawal just like it would if you were quitting heroin. Now if you have stopped for a day or two and not felt like you are experiencing discomfort, this can be normal too. It's usually when the body is starved of the substance and knows that it is not going to get it, that real withdrawal sets in. I have found that withdrawal is 2-part when it comes to Kratom. It is emotional (or psychological) as much as it is physical. Below are documented to be experienced by people who stop taking Kratom – I can attest to each and every one of these as it happened to me. I must be one of the unlucky ones in life!

- Insomnia or disturbed sleep (tossing and turning for weeks for me!)
- Headaches (dull persistent pain)
- Difficulty breathing – breathlessness (get out of breath quickly)
- Fatigue and lethargy that seems endless
- Muscle cramps and spasms (sometimes twitches)
- Lack of appetite (disinterest in food)
- Watering eyes or dry eyes that then water from being sensitive
- Increased anxiety or misplaced anxiety (feeling anxious when there's no reason)
- General sense of worry
- Depression or constantly feeling down and listless
- Unexpected anger or feelings of anger that sporadically crop up (mood swings)
- Hot flushes
- Fever-like symptoms
- Runny nose (almost like you have a cold)
- Extreme frustration with no way to relieve it
- Nausea and vomiting
- Restless legs (this was a KILLER for me)

- Flooding of all the emotional problems you have been putting off while using
- Cravings for Kratom (both mentally/emotionally and physically).

How many of these symptoms you experience seems to depend on how much Kratom you became reliant on every day, and how addicted you are to the substance.

Kratom withdrawals are much the same as regular opioid withdrawals but less intense. I find this to be the truth, but I must say that I have new-found respect for people who give up synthetic opioids successfully, because my Kratom withdrawal was pretty severe.

The withdrawal symptoms of Kratom start off mild at around 12 hours from your last dose. The brain will merely send out a gentle reminder that it is waiting for its dose. If you don't respond, it will gradually start increasing the severity of withdrawal symptoms. You can expect to experience withdrawal symptoms for approximately 10 to 15 days, with the worst of it peaking at around 5 days. This is when your brain and body is starting to realise that it's really not getting what it wants and needs to up its game.

While the severity of withdrawals will start to reduce from around day 10, in some cases, it can take weeks or months for a person to *feel* themselves again. The physical issues that the drug has brought about can take much longer. I am 8 months into recovery at writing this, and I am still suffering some pretty negative issues.

The Physical Issues Still With me 8 Months into Recovery

Let's talk shit: While my physical situation has improved drastically, I have only just seemed to push through the battle of constipation. I know, you probably don't want to hear about my poop schedule, but it's pretty important to talk about. If you were or are using as much as I was, your entire system can become really blocked up and you can get some pretty awful piles. Pooping floods of blood is not uncommon to serious Kratom users. I remember reading a Quitting Kratom post where a user sagely advised others still using that Kratom "will" ruin their lives and "will" make them pour buckets of blood from their butts. I was shocked and I also didn't believe it. Again; hindsight.

Up until this point, I have needed to take something to aid in getting my system working properly. I would say that things returned to a 'healthy' situation about 5 months into recovery, so I have stopped spending my money on Movicol, thank God!

The skin: In the final months of my Kratom use my skin was an absolute oil slick. It was greasy and shiny to such an extent that people were giving me unsolicited skincare advice. Since quitting, the oiliness has simply vanished. My skin has cleared up and there are no dark circles under my eyes. Yay! I believe that the dark circles only disappeared at about 3 months into recovery. This is also where my sleep patterns seemed to become more regular and I started getting more wholesome sleep – so that ties up quite nicely. People keep commenting on how "healthy" I am looking (they better not be referring to my weight gain!).

The hair: My hair (this is the biggest one for me), since quitting, has fallen out even more. I can only assume that if I was still using Kratom, it would be much more severe and probably impossible to hide, so there is some gratefulness within me. Just before I quit using Kratom, I noticed white patches of scalp showing through my hair. At first, I was shocked and obsessed over it. Then I noticed, to my horror that a *lot* of my hair was falling out. It really did start to become noticeable, especially on my forehead hairline area. I am a female in my early 30s and I have brown long hair. I do not have female pattern baldness in the family. I have noticed that there is some new "baby hair" growth to my relief. I will focus more on hairless further on, so if you are here to learn more about Kratom hair-loss, please note that I do cover it below.

The thyroid: My endocrine system and thyroid have been utterly distressed so I am on supplements in hopes that I can recover those. In reality, if those get back to a healthy functioning state, the hair should grow back and my skin should get even more healthy looking.

The weight: I am extremely thin and while I am eating more than I ever ate on Kratom, I don't seem to be putting on much weight. I currently weigh around 46kg.

The mind: Psychologically and emotionally, I feel as if I have been deserted by a best-friend. There's a void in my life. Because Kratom used to handle my emotions for me (take bad feelings away), I am now left to deal with these feelings on my own. I am always at risk of taking Kratom. As an addict, I am always in recovery. Sometimes I think about it and I have a sense of "it won't make a difference if I do it just once". The thing is; it will make a difference because it won't be just once. We all know that.

The legs: My restless legs, muscle cramps, and spasms didn't stop for a long time. They occurred at least weekly until around the 6th month of recovery.

The sexy time: My sex drive or libido is absolutely non-existent. At 6 months recovery, I had hoped to see a positive change as others had implied it took around that time. I am sorry to say… there's no change at all at 8 months in. Sex life obliterated – thanks Kratom. Let's hope for positive change in the future – other Kratom quitters have had success in rekindling their sexy time vibes, so don't feel distressed if you are new to quitting and have sex drive problems too.

THE POSITIVES OF QUITTING KRATOM

I realise that by mentioning all the negative impacts and physical discomforts of quitting Kratom that one might think there are no perks to kicking the habit. There are! Here's what I have experienced the most recent months of recovery already (and this is massive progress in my opinion).

- I no longer feel numb – feeling things, getting angry and having emotions may be uncomfortable but it's *something*. And it tells you that you are alive. Without these feelings (when Kratom removes them for you), you don't live reality and you miss out on a lot of things. Being deadpan is boring and it's an unauthentic way to live. Feel those emotions, get angry, get happy – ride the waves of the ups and downs. Feeling numb is no way to live. I didn't know this until I finally started feeling things again. It's funny because I had no idea I was actually numb to all of these things until I finally wasn't. My partner comments often on how much happier, wittier and perkier I seem.

- I *can* eat. I might not be putting on weight or sporting luscious sexy curves, but I can eat and the thought of it doesn't put me off. I often enjoy a good meal and don't find myself trying to find ways not to eat just so my Kratom can be more effective.

- My skin is clearer, smoother and dark eye-circle free! A few people have commented on how healthy I am looking.

- Lethargy and disinterest in the outside world has gone. I have enough energy to exercise and I find that I am interested in doing things. Those positive feelings go away so slowly when you are taking Kratom that you don't even notice it is happening. I exercise every day now and don't lose my breath as easily as I did before!

- I sleep and insomnia doesn't come for me unless I have a worry or stress, which is completely normal and not just drug-induced (as was the case when I was using Kratom).

- I feel happy and more myself. I actually enjoy life. I thought I didn't but I actually do.

- As I mentioned above, my balding head is seeing new baby hair growth. This is a massive inspiration/motivation to stay off the green powder. In fact, it is my main motivator. When I feel like being sneaky and having some Kratom, I think about how embarrassed I have been about my hair and that's enough to keep me clear of the stuff.

- My moods are more stable. When I was on Kratom and when I quit, I would find my moods to be quite temperamental. In the beginning I was calm and relaxed but the more my tolerance for the drug grew, the more temperamental my moods would be. Now, I do experience normal angers and happiness feelings, but I am more in control of them. No more angry or frustrated outbursts.

- I no longer need something to feel normal. I don't have to sneak to the bathroom, lie, or hide things.

- No more strange rashes, acid tongue or ulcers, or sore swollen gums.

- The whites of my eyes are in fact white and people have commented that my eyes look "wider" or more open. I have noticed this myself but I don't really know why it is the case.

- I can actually go the toilet – no problems!

I could write a list that spans many, many pages, but I think that I have made a valuable point already. Each and every day that goes by that I take my vitamins and supplements, eat a healthy diet, go to the gym or do some exercise – I get better. And I hope to fully recover eventually!

The Element of Surprise: Guess What, Kratom Has a Nifty Disguise

I would like to spend some time telling you a bit more about Kratom and what makes it the devilish plant it is, disguised as something good. Please don't get me wrong, I am not a Krater (my word for Kratom Hater), but I have experienced the full force of the plant and I wish to serve as a warning to those who are still in the honeymoon phase or the denial phase. Mark my words…Kratom will wreak its havoc on you. For some it will take mere weeks or years, for others it might take decades. But it *will* happen. I only hope that you make a positive change before the plant turns on you.

One thing I have learned is that even when a Kratom addict knows that their beloved plant is hurting them physically, they won't (and can't) admit it.

Kratom Informative – What You Need to Know About Kratom

Kratom addiction is formed after regular use. The problem is that the plant makes a user feel so good; it is hard to keep use down to an absolute minimum. Kratom makes changes to the brain's neural pathways and circuitry, which brings about a change in the way a person feels happy. Kratom floods the brain with the very same chemicals required for someone to feel happiness or pleasure. This means that once the body gets used to this new supplier of the happiness and pleasure feelings, when the external supplier is gone (no more Kratom) an individual can start to struggle to feel happiness and pleasure on their own. And thus, Kratom dependence forms.

- Kratom dosing effects

If you Google search "how to dose Kratom" you will probably be surprised to see how many user guides pop up offering advice for beginners. I did this when I first started with Kratom and it helped me to decide on a loose dosing plan that I could tweak until I found my "sweet spot". The thing about dosing with Kratom is that the drug affects the brain. And everyone's brain chemistry tends to be a little different. So what seems to be a massive dose and have crazy effects for one user might have minimal effects for another. Also, tolerance plays a role. I remember reading that 10 grams per day was a small dose and thinking "WTF, that's huge!" – yet in the end I was doing far more than that per day, so it's really about who you are as a person.

The average beginner will start with small doses to test things out. Most websites and user guides will recommend starting with 1 gram or 1.5 gram to see how it affects you. If you don't feel anything, they recommend increasing the dose. I remember that I started with half a gram, which is what gave me that lovely flood of great well-being feelings. I stayed on half a gram to around 2 grams per dose for at least 2 to 3 months. Then I began dosing 2 grams twice a day for around a month. My tolerance really did get bad at that point and I started taking 2 grams every 3 hours. And so the downward spiral began.

So my dosing schedule looked something like this:

First month/day	6 month / day	1 year / day	Final month/day
0.5 grams x 2	1.8 grams x 4	2.5 grams x 5	2.5 grams x 6 to 7

Keep in mind; I weighed about 53 kg at the time of starting with Kratom. I lost a whopping 11kg while taking Kratom daily.

When Kratom is ingested, the effects are typically felt within 15 to 20 minutes – 30 minutes in some instances (and depending on how much you have eaten prior). Depending on the strain (the quality), your weight, food consumed, and tolerance, it can last anything from around 2 hours to 5 hours. It all depends on the person and their unique situation.

Which brings me to the topic of tapering.

Quitting Kratom Using Tapering

- **I have recently come across some lovely Kratom tapering guides online. The best one can be found at (in my opinion) Kick Kratom – you can actually download a tapering schedule from there. Please note Kick Kratom is not affiliated to me in anyway and I am merely referencing them as an excellent source for Kratom tapering assistance.**

I must admit that I tried tapering to quit Kratom in the beginning, but I am just not strong enough to limit myself. I ended up doing my most recent quitting episode by going Cold Turkey and I can tell you that my mind set is far stronger now as a result. If you want to quite something, you need to be consistent and persistent with yourself. It's much like when you train a dog a new trick or behaviour. If you want to train a dog to sit before it gets dinner, you help it to sit before every meal. You are firm, repetitive and consistent. You don't let the dog sit sometimes and then let it do whatever it likes on some occasions. And so it is the same with me. I eventually had to take on this particular training method with myself. No slip ups allowed, no "just a little bit" situations – cold turkey was the name of the game for me in every sense of the term.

That being said, tapering wasn't completely useless to me. Tapering did in fact help me cut back to a point that I *could* actually go Cold Turkey without feeling like certain death was about to befall me. And that in itself is actually very valuable. So, I strongly believe that you can quit taking Kratom by tapering.

So, for those who don't know what tapering is – here goes. Tapering is a method of gradually reducing your dosage so that your body (and brain) doesn't have a complete freak out that it is no longer getting its fix. It's a way of tricking the body, but it's more than that too. It is also a way of being gentle and kind to yourself – allowing your body the time to slowly let go of one of its favourite vices and to gradually heal and strengthen to the point where it needs less and less of the drug it has become so accustomed to.

How I used tapering: My biggest advice with tapering is to apply a logical approach to how your specific body works. Grab a piece of paper and a pen and jot down how your Kratom journey took place. Rack your brain for the information – I know that it took a lot of work for me to remember. Write down how much you were taking and how frequently you were re-dosing from day one. Try to plot how your doses increased (or frequency) over the months until right now. You might notice a pattern emerge. Maybe you were increasing doses in 500mg increments or perhaps you were increasing at a slower pace. Now, use that information to plan your tapering schedule. This information will uncover how your body naturally grew dependent on Kratom and at what speed (or momentum).

It stands to reason – although I am no expert on the topic – that you can just as gradually start breaking that dependence at a similar, steady speed. Simply reverse your dosing schedule – well, that's what I did. Of course, you can go a little easy on yourself. The point is not to frighten your system or punish yourself but to make steady, realistic progress.

If you don't feel this is a viable method of tapering, there is a plethora of tapering schedules available online that you can try. I do personally stand by my method though and I sincerely hope that you will give tapering a try if you are hoping to quit.

Don't Just Taper… Taper with Purpose

Friedrich Nietzsche came up with a pretty valid quote that I feel applies to anyone wishing to quit anything. It goes "he who has a *why* to live for can bear almost any *how*". To me that speaks of purpose. If you have something to do and something to work towards, you will handle this process of tapering much better.

When it comes to tapering, you are going to notice a difference in how you feel mentally, emotionally and physically. It's a dangerous game to play to just trust the process. Your body and brain will be vaguely confused. And as an addict, you will be looking for ways to relinquish your steely approach, get bored, and just go have a dose.

And that's why it's important to incorporate some purpose into your life while you are tapering. Here's what worked for me...

Do something: It's a good idea to keep busy. So, while you are tapering, I recommend (strongly) learning a new skill, picking up a hobby, reading quit lit (these are books aimed at helping people quit addictions and they are **brilliant** for the recovering brain), starting an exercise routine (even a walking schedule is good). Just add something new to your life to go hand-in-hand with your tapering schedule. This might also give your brain something to blame its new found confusion on and hopefully it won't notice your taper too much! The powerful art of distracting your addicted brain is something I suggest you get comfortable with for a bit. I read a lot of quit lit and I am using an app to learn a new language.

Change what you do: As humans we tend to get stuck into little rituals without even thinking about it. Think about it now. When do you take the most Kratom? What are you doing while you take it? Are you listening to music? Are you off to the gym? The body and brain will have made a fairly strong link between the behaviour and the reward you were enjoying, so you need to get out of that. Change what you were doing when you were taking the Kratom. Try to avoid those scenarios.

Eat: Eat healthy! Yes, I know most of us don't want to eat anyway for some or other reason and I am not suggesting that you do a complete turnaround. Your body shouldn't be catapulted into a completely different lifestyle suddenly, but you are going to need to ensure that you are providing your body with a little something extra. You can expect some withdrawals. And nutrition is a good way to try to counteract some of the feelings you will have.

Kratom negatively impacts the endocrine system and the thyroid. It also completely messes up the digestive system. I would recommend getting supplements for the following: Omega 3 fatty acids, Vitamin B6 and B12, zinc, Iodine, and Vitamin C. Eat probiotic foods such as fresh herbs and coconut oil. And add to that a healthy supply of leafy greens, seeds and nuts, green beans, and pumpkin. I know, eating isn't easy or fun sometimes but think of a smoothie you can throw some of these things into, even if it's just once a day.

Connect: If you are quitting something and surrounded by people who aren't or people who don't understand the journey you are on, you may just fail. It is the very reason my first few attempts failed. You need to form part of a tribe. Your tribe needs to be people who are going through exactly the same thing as you, so don't go join AA or something vaguely related. Get specific. You will find Kratom Quitting groups online on Facebook as well as on Reddit. Get talking. Share your story, provide advice, get support and give support. You will be surprised at how having a tribe that is helping you and following your very same journey can help you to turn down a chug of the green powder when you really feel like it. I found my tribe on Reddit and I must admit that it really has kept me going. Thanks guys! I also strongly recommend speaking to a counsellor if you aren't opposed. It just helps you to be accountable for your addiction and the steps you are taking to fight it. Also, counsellors have a sneaky way of being able to help you put things into perspective.

Figure out the trigger: there's a reason that we backslide and relapse and that's because of triggers. The more we feel triggered, the more we seek out the thing that makes us feel better. If you have tried to quit before, make a list of all the times you went back to it even though you had promised yourself you wouldn't. Make a list and see if you can see a pattern. Obsess about it if you must, because there is a trigger usually and the sooner you figure out what that trigger is, the sooner you can eliminate it from your life (or at least try to).

QUITTING KRATOM COLD TURKEY

Before I went Cold Turkey, I got my Kratom use right down to 0.5 grams x 3 times per day. That's basically what I started on in the very beginning. Then one day, while I was sitting with a client, I rested my head in my hand. When I pulled my hand away, a chunk of hair was left behind. And that, for me, was all the motivation I needed to go Cold Turkey. I have not touched Kratom ever since. That was the very moment that I quit.

I must admit that going Cold Turkey is not easy. In fact, it is one of the most difficult things I have ever done in my life. I probably wouldn't have been able to do it if that chunk of hair didn't come out in my hand. It was a shocking experience. Any woman who has a chunk of her already thinning hair come out in her hand in front of an almost-stranger will be shocked. Horrified. Sickened. I threw up shortly after that happened. I then sat down and with a shaking hand I had to ask myself "what are you doing to yourself?". My next thought was "will my hair ever grow back!"

Tips for going Cold Turkey with Kratom dependence:

1. Determine your reason for starting Kratom in the first place so that you can work on an alternative. Did you start taking Kratom for pain? Or was it related to anxiety? Perhaps you have some deep-seated emotional problems that need to be worked out. Figure out your reason, because when you have the opportunity to slip up, the reason you started in the first place will be staring you in the face – and you won't know what to do. Once you know why, make sure you have a backup solution – just don't turn to another addictive drug, please.

2. Have strong resolve. Write down a list of reasons why you NEED to quit Kratom. Revisit this list every time you feel cravings or feel as if you are about to cave or slip up. The reasons on your list must really matter to *you*. Make them

deeply personal.

3. Set a goal. Some counsellors will tell you not to bargain with yourself. As a user, I say that's hogwash. Bargain with yourself, if it is what will get you out of the clutches of the Kratom plant. Plan a holiday, plan a fun evening or set up some sort of reward for yourself that you will ONLY get if you do in fact make it to a certain milestone. For me, I promised myself that if I made it 6 months clean, I would go on a weekend away to a beachy destination. During the 6 months leading up to this milestone, I had the reward firmly set in my mind and I worked on getting fit and bikini-ready. I also spent hours searching for things to do at the destination and plotted excursions and activities. I went on that holiday and it meant so much to me. The goal kept me busy – see where I'm going with this?

4. Join a fitness class, hire a personal trainer, or set yourself a workout schedule. There is nothing quite as effective as keeping yourself "otherwise occupied" when you are trying to quit something.

5. Join a tribe – much like when tapering, you need to find people who are going through the very same thing as you. When you have a question or a weak moment, your tribe will be there and you probably won't slipup. I have found many Kratom Quitting groups on social media platforms such as Facebook and Reddit.

6. Set an activity schedule. Cold Turkey is very different to tapering. There will be many hours where you will want your regular Kratom fix. A schedule will help you avoid those free moments where you could very easily have a quick dose. Line up binge-worthy series, buy quit lit books (books about quitting things), book appointments, set plans to visit someone or go the zoo, the park, the beach. Just make sure that you don't leave too much time free and available to

backslide – you don't need to do this forever, but I recommend being strategically busy for at least the first month or two.

7. Substitute. Rehab counsellors might disagree but luckily this book is just about *my* personal experience. I personally feel that it's helpful to substitute the addiction with something less harmful. For me this really worked. When I felt like having Kratom and the cravings set in, I would allow myself something else that is less harmful to myself. A cigarette, a cup of coffee, a creamy cappuccino, a bubble bath, a glass of wine (unless you are an alcoholic – then please don't do that), hours of funny cat videos – anything really.

Music: I found that the more I stayed away from Kratom, the more my love for music started to come back. I can now spend hours on YouTube watching music videos. Regardless of which quitting method you choose to go with, I would strongly recommend creating several playlists to suit the variety of mood swings you will undoubtedly have. You will experience a few mood swings and the best thing you can do is be prepared with something to mellow you out or lift your spirits. When I am bored, I spend hours on YouTube distracting myself with videos. And when I need to be doing daily tasks, but still need distraction from my cravings, I stick my earphones in and listen to music. My compilation of music playlists has a playlist saved for just about every mood. So you will find "bad mood", "depressed", "craving", "demotivated" labelled playlists on all my devices. It works for me. It could work for you too.

Write it out: I love to write and I find writing is a valuable form of therapy. This is the very reason why I am writing this book actually. You might not want to write anything to be published, but write about your experience. It will keep you busy and you might even want to share it with a loved one in the end. They will certainly appreciate the sharing.

The Rehab Route

I strongly recommend that anyone who is struggling with addiction seeks out the counsel and help of a rehab facility. The thing about rehabs is that they are never as bad as you think they are. They help you to realise the root cause of your addiction, you meet other people on the same or similar journey (you might make some life-long friends!) and best of all; they get you clean. Once you are over the hurdle of getting clean and surviving the withdrawals, you can focus on rebuilding your life and getting back to feeling okay.

Using Agmatine and Black Seed Oil – Viable or Not?

I personally am in two minds about using Agmatine and Black seed oil when tapering or quitting Kratom. I did quite a bit or reading to find out why people use Agmatine in the first place. I have read that Agmatine can help decrease a person's tolerance when taking Kratom. Although most other reports I have read have been quite adamant that Agmatine is helpful in reducing withdrawal symptoms. Here's what I have gleaned from my readings (I have done a lot of that):

- Agmatine, when tested on animals, is able to inhibit opioid dependence and also reduce the instances of relapse.
- Agmatine relieves withdrawal symptoms of opiates and alcohol.

On the topic of Blackseed oil… Black seed oil, or nigella sativa, is known as potentiator for Kratom effects. This means that it makes it a bit better…but there's also information that points to Black seed oil staving off withdrawals. I have also read that it has some mild opioid effects of its own. Hmmm, like I said before, I am in two minds about using these when tapering or quitting Kratom. I personally would choose to avoid taking anything that I was using with Kratom to get to that nice sweet spot. For me, recovery is quite emotional and psychological, so I think the association with the Agmatine and Black seed oil with Kratom would be a bit overwhelming.

Kratom Hair Loss – Why it Happens, What to Expect, & What to do About it

Here's the clincher. Dun dun dunnnn...... Kratom causes hair loss. Sorry nay-sayers, I have spoken to too many ex users and experienced it myself for your nay-saying to have effect.

If you are reading this because you want to learn more about Kratom hair loss, then I cannot help but say that my feelings are with you. I have suffered hair thinning and hair loss thanks to Kratom.

When I was using Kratom and just after I stopped, I thought of every possible reason why my hair could be falling out and disappearing that *isn't* related to Kratom use. I checked out every possible option from my birth control pill to my diet. Some people on forums told me to check my thyroid which is something I have never had issues with before. And that is where I made an interesting connection. I had in fact developed a thyroid problem due to a stressed endocrine system and Kratom does in fact do this. I have spoken to many other Kratom users who have suffered hair loss. In fact, before writing this, I made it my mission to track Kratom users who suffered hair loss or hair thinning, and the result was astounding. Many, many Kratom users have this problem. Now that I have stopped Kratom, the hair is slowly growing back.

Now if you are a naysayer and don't believe that Kratom causes hair loss, I hear you. The information that I have found does indicate that hair loss doesn't affect everyone. It affects many, many people though. Also, it really depends on how long and how much you are using.

I have noticed from sharing information with others that the pattern of hair loss is very similar in all of us. The hair generally seems to thin all over – almost as if there are no filler hairs. You may start to see a bit more scalp than you are used to seeing. In the beginning, like me, you may even notice this but think nothing of it, because it is not highly visible. The next thing I noticed was the hair along my hairline in front (so the forehead area) – that started thinning rather dramatically. I now like to wear a beanie as you can see right through the hairs and it really doesn't look great. The next was almost chunks of hair falling out on either side of the "widow's peak" area of my hair. That is probably the area where my hair loss is the most extreme and it almost appears as if I have male pattern baldness. Ahem! I am **not** a man! The thing that scares me the most is that when I first noticed weird thinning in my hair, I continued to use Kratom and hoped for the best. I remember thinking to myself, "how bad can it really get?". Don't play this game guys, it can get pretty bad!

Here's what one can assume about Kratom (note this is not scientific research, but based on many studies I have read and professionals spoken to).

- Kratom can have an impact on a person's TSH/T4.
- Some Kratom supplies can contain heavy metals.
- Some studies show that high doses of indole alkaloid mitragynine may reduce how the thyroid gland responds to TSH (thyroid stimulating hormone) which results in primary hypothyroidism. The National Center for Biotechnology Information, which is part of the United States National Library of Medicine, actually did research into this.

I have been nearly digitally crucified on pro-Kratom forums for bringing this up. Some Kratom users are firmly against this theory, but it's surely no co-incidence that so many users are losing their hair.

T4: This is a thyroid hormone called Thyroxine. This hormone needs to be produced by the body to assist with growth and metabolism. If you become ill or take a chemical/substance that inhibits or causes an overproduction of T4, you may notice things like hair loss, weight loss, lack of appetite, dry eyes, insomnia, skin dryness, anxiety, fatigue, sensitivity to cold. Does any of this sound familiar? It certainly does to me. This sounds like an almost perfect description of me just a few months ago.

TSH: Thyroid stimulating hormone affects the functioning of the thyroid. Kratom may slow the production of this hormone, which helps the body regulate how it uses its energy. It also helps with regulating mood, muscle strength, and body temperature. The result of a deficiency is: hair loss, dry skin and scalp, brittle nails, constipation, tiredness, inability to tolerate the cold, irregular menstruation. Again, does this sound familiar to you?

You can go for a thyroid test when you quit Kratom to ascertain if your use of the plant has contributed to your hair loss by causing thyroid hormone issues. There are medications that you can be given by the doctor to assist the thyroid to return to normal functioning. I have done a lot of reading online and have come to the conclusion that when you completely stop taking Kratom, the hair can grow back, but it doesn't happen immediately. For some people it takes a while longer for things to go back to normal.

How long will hair loss be a problem?

When you quit Kratom, hair loss seems to continue to happen for a few weeks and then stops. This doesn't mean that it starts reversing straight away. What I noticed was that it continued to thin and fall out for over a month after I quit Kratom. Then, it stopped and remained the same for at least 5 months. It should then take between 4 and 6 months to start seeing new baby hair growth. This seems to be standard across the board, but there are a few people who have to wait longer to see this.

The good news is that you can naturally spruce up your thyroid functioning, if you don't wish to visit a doctor or take specialised medication. Unfortunately, you cannot take these products while still using Kratom and hope for a miracle. You will need to eliminate the cause of the problem and that is the Kratom. Then start to supplement.

Some tips for caring for your hair when quitting Kratom:

- Take a very good multivitamin.
- Take biotin.

- Supplement your magnesium intake.
- Supplement your Omega 3, 6 and 9 in-take.
- Take Iodine supplement (you don't need to take this every day).
- Invest in a tub or bottle of natural coconut oil. Comb this into your hair at least twice a week and sleep with it in. Don't forget to condition your hair.
- Exercise regularly.

I know many reading his probably have minimal to zero interest in eating healthy meals and exercising – who wants to do that right? I certainly didn't. BUT, I can tell you that the vast improvements I have noticed in my appearance lately have been due to a healthy balanced diet and exercise 3 times a week. On the plus side, not only do I look better (people keep complimenting me, yay!), but I also feel less lethargic and I feel happy in my mind set. No antidepressants required for me!

How to Heal Your Kratom Induced Thyroid Problems

I would strongly suggest going for a thyroid test when quitting Kratom. If there is serious stress on the system, a doctor can provide you with the right type of supplements and medication. If you are anything like me, you probably don't want to see a doctor. You can find over the counter Thyroid support supplements at fairly cheap prices. I did that and I pop one capsule every day. You can also incorporate thyroid-friendly foods in your diet such as:

- Salt (make sure it is Iodized salt)
- Magnesium (take a supplement or eat spinach and lettuce) – remember that Magnesium is better absorbed when you have healthy vitamin D levels, so get out into the sun for a half hour each day or pop a vitamin D tablet.
- Seafood
- Nuts
- Kale
- Soy (don't overdo it on the soy).

Keep in mind that there is no quick fix. It could take months for you to get back to normal, but you will feel great when you do! Be consistent in your approach to boosting your health after quitting Kratom.

With a thyroid problem you will feel tired (fatigued), weak, out of breath, cold (more so than other people), lack an appetite, and even be constipated. Muscle cramps and aches are also common. These symptoms will gradually go away as your thyroid bounces back to health. Trust me – just give it time. Be patient.

Kratom and Sexy Time Obliteration

As you know, Kratom wreaked havoc with my sex drive. I quite literally went from a person with an extremely high sex drive to have completely no interest in it at all. It got quite bad. I don't find men attractive and it's extremely difficult for my partner to get me in the mood for sexy time (wink wink). This means that a lot of the time, panic exists around the issue and also, one has to pretend to be interested, which as you know is not ideal. So why does this happen. Well, it still comes down to the endocrine system and how the thyroid functions.

I have also read a plethora of posts where Kratom users confirm that they have a total lack of sex drive while using the substance. It's a difficult task finding too much medical information online, but what I did find was that some opioids and pain medications can reduce a person's libido or make it completely disappear while using the medication. One can deduce that because Kratom works on the very same receptors in the brain that pain medications and opioids do, that it too can negatively impact on the libido. Most ex users who have reported loss of libido while using Kratom do get it back when they quit. I haven't – where is mine? I don't know.

After doing extensive research I have come to the following conclusions. The thyroid can affect sex drive and we all know where I stand in that department. If you have a Kratom related thyroid issue, try to fix that problem first. Something else that I read was that testosterone influences sex drive in both men and women. Without getting too much into the nitty gritty of progesterone, testosterone and oestrogen in men and women… I have noted that both men and women need testosterone to feel eager for sexy time. Taking a mild testosterone supplement on a daily basis for a few weeks might be a good way to boost your libido. This is something that is recommended to both men and women who suffer libido issues, so it's worth a try. Don't overdo it though.

Kratom & Digestive Problems

When you use Kratom a lot and for a long time, you don't get away without a few painful constipation experiences. For some users, like me, it may even seem like you are dying! The thing with Kratom is that it slows down the bowel and digestive system. It's not a serious condition, but can become serious if it is persistent. Because of discomfort and a slowed system, bowel movements become extremely infrequent. This can lead to colon problems and result in ruptures if the user doesn't take preventative measures. The constipation is expected to cease as soon as Kratom use stops, but this is unfortunately not the case. Your body won't be used to processing food normally and when you quit Kratom, it will continue as per normal for a few weeks, at least. It took a few months for things to get back to normal for me.

Kratom and Anorexia

When I was in my prime of taking Kratom, people kept commenting "wow you have gotten thin", "OMG, are you okay, you look sick you are so thin", "eat something!" and so on. At the time, it was quite flattering, but I wasn't really seeing myself realistically. My clothes had become baggy, I was stick thin and the thought of food was far from my mind. I was thin, yes, but I didn't look particularly pretty.

Kratom undoubtedly causes weight-loss. In some instances, users have progressed to full blown eating disorders such as Anorexia. When a person insists on a low-calorie diet (the less you eat, the better the Kratom effects), the body will experience quick and serious weight loss which ultimately puts the internal organs at risk of failure. If someone already has Anorexia and uses Kratom, the Kratom will stave off feelings of hunger which puts the victim at even more risk, in my opinion.

HOLISTIC NATURAL SUPPLEMENTS TO EASE KRATOM CRAVINGS

While I was doing a bit of research and reading on Reddit, I noticed a few people were asking if there are natural supplements and vitamins that one can take to ease Kratom cravings. Before I get started, it is important to note that there is no official food and drug administration approved vitamins and supplements for use in opiate detoxification and withdrawal. However, there are many survivors who speak of the supplements and vitamins that they have used and some researchers and doctors have recommended various things over the years. I am glad that I can share this list with you. And here it is!

- Multi-vitamin.
  This is a bit of a no-brainer, but if you don't take any vitamins already, try to get your hands on a good multi-vitamin. Coming off opiates almost always means you have nutritional deficiencies, so getting your nutrients and vitamins intake in order is the first step.

- Passionflower.
  Passionflower is quite well known for treating anxiety. There are studies out there that say people who have used clonidine for opiate withdrawal with Passionflower have enjoyed quite a bit of relief from the physical symptoms of withdrawal. Something to consider…

- Ginseng.
  Okay, don't rush out and buy ginseng if you have cancers as it can cause complications. Ginseng has been used by many people going through opiate withdrawal as it helps to quell anxiety. Don't use just any Ginseng. Look out for Red Ginseng. If you take too much you could get a speedy heartbeat, dry mouth and more time on the toilet.

- Acetyl-L-carnitine.

If you have every used this supplement before, you will know that it is great for muscle recovery and for a good night's sleep. During opiate withdrawal you are probably going to feel irritable, restless, and have insomnia, so this can really help in terms of that. Again, if you are taking any cancer drugs, don't take this without chatting to your doctor as it can cause complications.

- Vitamin C.
  Here's the interesting thing about Vitamin C. The NCBI released a study that was done using high doses of vitamin C to help stave off withdrawal symptoms in heroin users. You can read the study here. Apparently, it helped with withdrawals at very high doses. Don't worry – it's not toxic if you take a lot. At worst, you might spend a bit of extra time on the toilet!

Some other supplements to look into that I don't personally affiliate myself with include: Rhodiola Rosea 3% Rosavin, 5-HTP, L-Theanine, and Bacopa.

DOCTOR PRESCRIBED MEDICATIONS OFTEN USED IN RECOVERY

I am told that doctor's prescriptions and rehab facilities can vary in terms of their treatments but reports I have seen infer that some recommend targeting withdrawal symptoms with:

- Antidepressants
- Anxiolytic medication (anti-anxiety)
- Anti-inflammatories (non-steroidal)
- Lofexidine (blood pressure medication)
- Dihydrocodeine (opioid pain reliever)

The risk of depression and suicidal thoughts

Unfortunately, depression is a reality for many of us. In fact, one of the reasons I enjoyed Kratom was because while using it, I no longer needed my anti-depressants. I was taking Lorien and it gave me a sort of mellow head fog that I hated. On Kratom, I had such a great sense of well-being that I never needed them.

When quitting Kratom, especially if you are struggling with depression or using Kratom to alleviate it, you can expect to be flooded with depressive feelings and suicidal thoughts. I would never advise anyone to just "power through". If you are feeling seriously bad, I strongly recommend seeing your doctor about an anti-depressant. Even if you don't want to take them long term, some doctors can give you a prescription to help you make through the worst of the withdrawal period. Depression and anxiety is a real thing. I have experienced it myself in mammoth proportions from time to time – so don't wait. And if you feel helpless and alone, pick up the phone, call a friend or family member. Heck, look me up on Reddit and message me long into the night.

I have read some advice on things to take for depression while quitting Kratom. Here's what I found:

- L-Tryptophan.
  500mg doses twice a day seems to be the norm.

- L-Tyrosine.
  500mg doses once a day seems the norm.

- L-Phenylalanine.
  500mg also seems to be the norm once or twice per day.

I can't speak of the safety or effectiveness of any of these, this is just a quick peak at what I have found other people are using. The best advice I can give on depression is to keep busy and of course, get an anti-depressant from your local doctor.

STARE RELAPSE IN THE FACE | MANAGING RELAPSE

As a Kratom addict you are probably regularly worried about relapse. That's the thing. We are all at risk of relapsing at any time. I once read a post by a poor girl who had made it 11 months into recovery and then relapsed. She took it so badly and seemed unable to reconcile her thoughts and go back to healthy living.

Relapsing is part of life. I have a theory that you need to stare it in the face. All a relapse aims to do is bring you down and discredit all the good, hard work that you have done. If you relapse, own it. Then pick yourself up and start from where you were. There's no reason to discredit yourself. The only thing you need to do is be honest about it. Tell someone. Be accountable. Make sure that someone knows you are having a weak moment or two. When someone knows, accountability seems to pique. Trust me on that one. Also, go read through my tips again on quitting. It never hurts to refresh your memory and get back into the right quitters mind set.

The End, or is it?

I would like to say that my relationship with Kratom is over and that I will never dabble with it again. I would be bold to say that. I don't want to touch the drug, but as an addict, I am always at risk. I believe that the plant is a pure mistress of evil in my life that seeks to destroy all that is genuinely good by momentarily distracting me with a false sense of well-being. I believe in strength in numbers and I want to be a support system for any and all who are struggling to quit or who have quit Kratom. This was my story – I would love to hear yours.

FRANKFORT FREE LIBRARY
123 Frankfort St.
Frankfort, NY 13340
(315) 894-9611

A1309028
362.293 SAF
Safari Girl.
My Kratom hell :

Made in the USA
Monee, IL
09 July 2021

Frankfort Free Library
0004800281000